Ethereum & Ether.

MW00887431

Pgs 42-43 Maker is , . . . "stablecoin"

Insurance & Blockchain p. 44

CoinBase - exchange where buy coins

# Ethereum: The Ultimate Guide To The World Of Ethereum

EEA - Enterprise Ethereum Alliance p. 85

### Ikuya Takishima

p 16) The Vevue Project - Google Street View
⌐> 4G Capital - Concept Daap providing instant access to capital and credit for small businesses in Africa

CoinDesk - a leading blockchain news site

Hardware Wallets for coin storage p. 70
⌐ basically specialized USB stick

ISBN: 1978012373
ISBN-13: 9781978012370

# TABLE OF CONTENTS

# Introduction

Welcome to my book, Ethereum: The Ultimate Guide To The World of Ethereum! First of all, thank you for purchasing this book. Secondly, congratulations on taking this step toward learning more about this network and its currency. Ethereum is set to change the way we manage processes across all industries and Ethereum's currency is potentially very profitable. It's an exciting moment for Ethereum and those involved in it. In this book, we will look in more detail at why Ethereum is a revolutionary technology and what this means in investment terms.

Are you looking to invest in a cryptocurrency that has the potential to reap high levels of profits? Do you want to know more about the technology that could convert centralized systems across thousands of services into open source, decentralized networks? This technology is Ethereum, and it is one of the most talked about crypto-technologies of the moment, alongside its currency, known as Ether. This book is going to provide you with everything you need to know about Ethereum and whether it is worth investing in now.

Like many people, I became interested in Bitcoin years ago, when Bitcoin was still relatively new, but hinting at a huge profit margin for those who took the risk and invested. It was after a couple of years playing around on the Bitcoin market that I heard about a new type of blockchain technology, one that wasn't just a digital form of payment, but one that could support potentially endless different types of applications. Not only that, but it comes with its own currency. This, to me, sounded like a potentially profitable situation, so I decided to dig a little deeper.

Unlike Bitcoin, Ethereum is still largely unknown to those who don't keep up with the cryptocurrency world, so the amount of information available is limited or highly technical. Still, it was fascinating and the more I read about Ethereum, the more I began to see its huge potential. And I'm not alone. More and more Fortune 500 companies are investing in Ethereum technology as it becomes increasingly lucrative and poises to change business processes as we know them.

I decided to condense my research and share my knowledge on Ethereum by writing this book. The book is designed for those who are new to cryptocurrency, but want to invest in it or learn more about it, as well as for more experienced traders looking to expand their portfolios. With a 5,000% increase in value in the first few months of 2017, Ethereum is proving to be a profitable currency. Still, as it is so new – it was only launched in 2015 – it comes with many infancy-related risks. It's partly this that makes it so exciting. This book will help you make your own investment decisions and decide if Ethereum is the right coin for you after weighing up the pros and cons that are presented here.

So far, Ethereum has made me good money and I was

lucky to make the investment when I did. However, now is not too late to invest, not by a long shot. In fact, now is the perfect moment to make the most of Ethereum's infancy and gain potential first-mover advantages. Ethereum's technology is only at the beginning of its potential growth stages, possibly reaching to dozens of industries and thousands of services. If its technology is adopted the way it is expected to be, Ethereum will enjoy a long and lucrative spot at the top. The profits are ripe for the taking.

Without further ado, let's learn more about Ethereum. The first question on everyone's mind is: what exactly is Ethereum? Let's take a look in the first chapter.

Happy reading!

# Chapter 1: What Is Ethereum?

In this chapter, we will look at what Ethereum is and where it came from. To understand what Ethereum is, we first need to understand blockchain technology.

Blockchain technology is what makes Ethereum – and Bitcoin – work. When Bitcoin was first launched, the idea of an online payment system that worked using digital currency rather than traditional fiat money was seem as modern and exciting. However, what should have been recognized as the real star of this invention was the technology behind Bitcoin, the platform that made it all happen. This platform is known as blockchain technology.

The blockchain system runs on the internet. Unlike the World Wide Web, however, blockchain technology is decentralized, open, and cryptographic. It allows a network of trust that runs on peer-to-peer transactions. This has created new security benefits that could never be imagined in centralized networks. Hacking a centralized intermediary is possible for someone with the skills and knowledge to do so; hacking a block in the blockchain is far more difficult.

The blockchain is basically a decentralized database that keeps millions of records of transactions that take place digitally. It doesn't have any kind of central administrator as conventional databases have, such as the databases stored at banks and government offices Instead, it has a complex network of repeated databases that anyone in the network community can see.

Blockchain technology is largely linked to Bitcoin, as it is the main and first application in the network. However, it actually has many other uses and several hundred different applications besides Bitcoin use blockchain technology as a platform to operate from.

Ethereum is one of them.

To put it simply, Ethereum is a type of open software platform that runs on blockchain technology. Creating blockchain applications used to be a complex process, requiring advanced knowledge in math, coding, and cryptocurrency. However, Ethereum is changing this. Its platform is not just for cryptocurrency, it also provides tools and means for developers to create other decentralized applications, such as regulatory compliance and electronic voting, among many others.

So, while it may use the same technology as Bitcoin and shares some similar uses, it also has its own unique characteristics.

# How Does Ethereum Compare To Bitcoin?

First of all, they are both blockchain networks that are distributed publicly. That is the key similarity between the two. Besides this, they are quite different. There is a distinct technical difference between them related to their purpose and their capability. Using blockchain technology, Bitcoin offers one specific application – an online payment network that operates using a peer-to-peer system and enables Bitcoin transactions to be made. In other words, it is a truly digital currency that operates around the world. The main purpose of the Bitcoin blockchain is to track and record transactions and ownership of bitcoins. Ethereum, on the other hand, has more far-reaching capabilities. Not only does it operate a cryptocurrency system – its cryptocurrency is known as Ether – it also focuses on running any given code for any other types of decentralized application.

In other words, Ethereum allows computer applications to run on its network that have nothing to do with cryptocurrency.

This is Ethereum's major advantage and most exciting feature. The main appeal of Bitcoin is that currency is not controlled by a leading central party nor is it a part of a central server. Ethereum has this feature and also allows other applications to operate on its network in the same way.

Why is this so exciting? Take, for example, a cloud storage system. On a centralized network, you trust a central server to manage it for you and take responsibility for it. On a decentralized network, your cloud system depends on others who are using it and who have an interest in making it work and keeping it maintained.

Nowadays, numerous applications are being built on Ethereum. It is also helping start-ups raise money with initial coin offerings. With its multi-purpose network and ability to provide a platform that gives ample space to developers, Ethereum is soaring in popularity. It's currently the second most valuable payment method, only just behind the original Bitcoin.

Miners don't mine for bitcoins in the Ethereum blockchain; instead, they work to get Ether. Ether is the cryptocurrency that operates on the Ethereum network. As well as being a tradeable cryptocurrency, application developers also use it to pay for any services or transaction fees that occur on the Ethereum network. Instead of being a true cryptocurrency in the sense Bitcoin is, Ether is more the fuel to support the various transactions and exchanges on the Ethereum network. However, Ether can still be traded on global exchanges and many traders make good profits this way.

Its popularity can be seen in the numbers. Its value has increased by 2,300% since 2015, with a 5,000% increase in the first few months of 2017, and one Ether is now worth nearly $290.

So, how did Ethereum come to be? And how did it become so popular? Let's take a look at its history.

# The History Of Ethereum

The first mention of Ethereum was in 2013 by the 19-year-old Russian programmer, Vitalik Buterin, who was also involved in the development of Bitcoin. He talked about Ethereum in a white paper with the aim of creating decentralized apps, a capability that Bitcoin lacked. In this paper, he argued that what Bitcoin needed was a specific scripting language that would allow application development on its platform

However, he didn't gain a general consensus with his ideas and Bitcoin was created with the sole purpose of being a cryptocurrency payment system. Undeterred, Buterin created a new proposal of developing a platform with a wider and more general scripting language. He set to work developing it alongside a team of three other programmers in 2014. It was launched in 2015.

There have been issues raised about Ethereum's scalability and security, but these are constantly being worked on through something called milestones. Milestones are planned protocol upgrades that aim to improve the functionality and incentive structures of the platform.

An important part of Ethereum is Ether, the value token (or in other words, the currency) of the network. It plays a significant role on the blockchain as it is used for paying transaction fees and services in Ethereum. Despite Ethereum's extraordinary success, Ether can be volatile in nature. While it can be volatile, Ether's value has overall increased, especially in 2017, and looks set to maintain a stable value. It's these kind of movements and patterns on the market that have captured media attention and investor interest, thrusting the Ethereum network into the spotlight and creating a new potential threat to Bitcoin.

## Chapter Summary

In this chapter, we looked at what Ethereum is and how it compares to Bitcoin. We also learned about blockchain technology, which is basically a decentralized system that allows transactions and exchanges to occur without any need for a central authority or for a governing body.

- Although often compared, Bitcoin and Ethereum have very different purposes and capabilities. Bitcoin is a pure cryptocurrency and its blockchain is designed to make financial transactions. While Ethereum also has a cryptocurrency – known as Ether – this is to pay for services on the Ethereum network. Also, Ethereum's blockchain is far superior to that of Bitcoin as it is capable of supporting thousands of applications that have many different functions.

- Ethereum was launched in 2015 and was first mentioned by Vitalik Buterin in a white paper.

- Ether is the currency of Ethereum. It is volatile by nature, but it plays a crucial part in facilitating the flow of the Ethereum network. It also enjoyed enormous increases in value over the last few months, making it an attractive investment option.

In the next chapter, we will look at some important aspects of the Ethereum network. These are smart contracts, Dapps, and DAOs. These elements are important because they set Ethereum apart from other systems that operate on blockchain technology. They also enable the development of the potentially thousands of different programmes that can run on the Ethereum platform.

# Chapter 2: Smart Contracts, Dapps, And DAOs

In this chapter, we will look at the use, purpose, and function of Ethereum in more detail and introduce the concepts of smart contracts, DAOs, Dapps, and other important aspects.

## What Are Smart Contracts?

Smart contracts run on the blockchain and operate within a decentralized system. They are also known as digital contracts, self-executing contracts, or blockchain contracts. Using the blockchain, the idea was formed that contracts could be digitalized by transforming them into a computer code. They could then be stored and replicated on the blockchain and managed by the network. In other words, rather than having a paper contract, it is digitalised on the blockchain. The contract code is programmed to automatically fulfil the clauses and terms in the contract, eliminating the need for a central authority to manage it.

Thanks to Ethereum's capability of supporting several applications, it is possible to run smart contracts on their blockchain. There are other blockchains that can also support smart contracts, but Ethereum is undoubtedly the most advanced.

Basically, "smart contract" is the term used to describe a computer code that enables exchanges of things of value, such as money, shares, property, and information. It can run on the blockchain and actually functions as a self-operating program that will accomplish tasks automatically, provided that certain conditions and stages are met. It eliminates the need to use an intermediary or a middle man, saving time, money, and potential conflicts of interest.

The process is far simpler than using conventional methods. Traditionally, a lawyer or notary would be used to get a specific document, before having to make a payment for their services and then waiting for the process to be completed. Smart contracts have a different strategy. You pay using cryptocurrency on the ledger (or the blockchain) and you receive your document instantly.

Smart contracts are versatile and can be used for several different purposes and under various circumstances. These include property law, legal processes, financial derivatives, insurance premiums, and breach contracts. They can be encoded on any blockchain. However, thanks to its unlimited processing capability, it is most common to use Ethereum for smart contracts.

Let's look at some examples of what we can use smart contracts for:

> Voting during political elections. Using smart contracts would provide an even more secure system for voting than what exists now and would make it almost impossible to rig. There are two main advantages that would come about from using smart contracts for voting. The first is the huge amount of security it provides. Hacking the system would require votes to be decoded, which in itself requires tremendous computer power, making it incredibly difficult to falsify. Finally, it would encourage more people to vote, as it would simply be online and would let people avoid the hassle of having to physically show up at a polling place to vote.

> Smart contracts can be used in organizations as a communication and workflow tool. Its streamlined process means it cuts through the need to wait for approvals and issues to be resolved. Its accuracy also reduces the chance of general human error.

> It can be used in the world of real estate. Using a ledger can reduce overall costs by removing the need to pay for a middleman to advertise the rental property and taking the need for

someone to confirm the transactions out of the equation. By buying through Ethereum or Bitcoin, the property contract can be encoded in the blockchain. The contract would remain there permanently and it would be impossible for someone to tamper with its clauses.

➤ Smart contracts could totally change the face of healthcare. The blockchain could be used to store private health records and only individuals with a specific private key could access them. It could also facilitate insurance claims by storing surgery and prescription receipts on the blockchain and automatically sending these to the insurance providers. This would provide a systematic and straightforward way of dealing with claims that can become time-consuming and loaded with paperwork.

➤ Smart contracts can be used in medical research. For example, in the case of cancer research, smart contracts can be used to easily share cancer data by facilitating the patient consent management process while protecting the privacy of the patients and their healthcare records at the same time. The data shared on the smart contracts can facilitate data contribution and allow easier cross-comparisons between researchers.

As we have covered, a key function and purpose of Ethereum is to create a platform that multiple applications can operate from. Although cryptocurrency is a part of this and it does provide a way of making digital payments, as we now understand, this is not the only thing Ethereum does or is capable of doing.

Here are some of the advantages of smart contracts:

> Smart contracts give autonomy, as it leaves the individual responsible for making the contract. There is no need for a lawyer or any kind of intermediary to be involved. As the tasks are fulfilled and accomplished on the network, it completely removes third party bias.

> Smart contracts create an atmosphere of trust and obligation. As the documents are encrypted on the blockchain, it is impossible for them to be lost, as they exist on a shared system. It is also practically impossible to tamper with them, as all changes are recorded on the blockchain and need to be validated.

> Documents on the blockchain are duplicated several times, so it is almost impossible to lose them.

> Blockchains are built on cryptography, which is a complex system that is incredibly hard to hack. It means that smart contracts are stored in a very safe environment.

> Automation in the system speeds up the process and eliminates the need to spend time and effort on manually preparing documents.

Smart contracts are both time effective and financially efficient.

➢ It also saves money, as there is no need to pay an intermediary, which can often become very expensive.

➢ Smart contracts are automated, which means they tend to be more accurate than manually-filled and organized documents.

Smart contracts are one of the best and most exciting aspects of blockchain technology. They have the potential to revolutionize the way we perform tasks associated with bureaucratic processes that include everything from healthcare to insurance. However, there are still some flaws in the system and smart contracts still have some issues to overcome.

Here are some of the possible drawbacks of smart contracts:

➢ The code is encrypted in such a way that it makes it very hard for hackers to get in. However, like any digital system, it could still get bugs that have grave consequences for the blockchain. Care has to be taken to produce contracts without any flaws. Once the contract is in the system, it is hard to change and it will continue to function the way it has been input into the system, even with faults.

➢ Smart contracts raise questions about regulation. As they operate within a decentralized system, there is no central authority or main leader. This makes it unclear how the government could or should regulate it and how they would tax transactions. These concerns could prevent the apps from growing as quickly as they could.

➢ Problems could occur if the wrong code is sent, as the transactions are automatic and irreversible. In the case of a traditional contract, issues can be dealt with in court. In the case of the blockchain, the contract will complete its role independent of the situation.

➢ In some industries, such as the financial industry, knowing who the customer is and their financial background is an important part of this industry to help prevent crime such as money laundering. However, in a system that operates in a decentralised nature, smart contracts remove the requirement of having customer information. This raises questions as to how crimes such as money laundering and fraud could be managed.

Another important part of Ethereum is the Ethereum Virtual Machine, otherwise shortened to EVM.

# What Is EVM?

The Ethereum Virtual Machine is a software that runs on the Ethereum network and lets anyone run any type of program. It makes the process of creating applications much easier and more efficient than it was in the past and this is one of the main advantages of Ethereum. It basically allows the development of up to thousands of different applications on one platform instead of needing to create a completely new blockchain for every new app. It means that even novice developers can attempt to make applications, as the structure is far simpler than it was before.

It is one of the most important parts of Ethereum, as it gives it the capability to support so many different apps. It allows developers to create, develop, and install decentralized applications on the blockchain.

What are decentralized applications?

Decentralized applications – or Dapps, as they are otherwise known as – are apps that serve a specific purpose. An example of a Dapp is Bitcoin. Its purpose is to provide a peer-to-peer cash system that allows its users to make online Bitcoin payments.

Dapps run on blockchain networks. This means, like the blockchain itself, Dapps are not controlled by any central authority. Dapps are not limited to cash systems. In fact, any centralized service can be converted into a Dapp using Ethereum, which opens new doors for services across almost all industries. These include loans, title registries, regulatory compliance, and voting systems.

But it's not just services that are using Dapps. There are quite a few other exciting new projects being built on the Ethereum blockchain right now. The Vevue project, for example, aims to bring Google street view to life. It enables its users to take short clips of places and share it with the world, building a collection of real-time video clips to create an interactive and moving picture of the world. Other projects include Etheria, a blockchain technology version of Minecraft which allows players to construct things and farm for items. As it is built on the decentralised network, it is not owned by a single entity, but instead it's a collaboration between all the players. It means it cannot be censored nor can it be removed by anyone, not even the government.

Other interesting uses of Dapps include 4G Capital, a concept Dapp that provides instant access to capital and credit for small business in Africa. Donors can use the app to fund small African businesses using digital currency. The idea is to empower these businesses through financial means and help promote change in Africa. Another use that helps show the diversity of Dapps is Ampliative Art, a kind of social network-platform that allows artists to organise their own art galleries and exhibitions for free. Artists can get exposure to their work and reap rewards through donations, comments, reviews, and feedback.

Decentralized Autonomous Organizations can also be built on the Ethereum network.

# What Are Decentralized Autonomous Organizations?

Decentralized Autonomous Organizations are also known as DAOs. As the name suggests, they are decentralized organizations without a central authority or leader. They operate on programming code that exists on a group of one or more smart contracts that are encoded on the Ethereum blockchain. Like the blockchain, the code of a DAO moves away from the traditional organization by removing any requirement for centralized control and people power. Not even the original developer of the DAO has any extra authority, and it runs independently without the need for intervention. It's funded by a group of individuals that cover its basic costs and give the funders voting rights rather than any kind of ownership or equity shares. This creates an autonomous and transparent system that will continue on the network for as long as it provides a useful service for its customers.

So now we know more about Dapps and DAOs, let's take a look at some of their pros and cons.

Here are some of the benefits of decentralized applications:

> They are independent, so no person or other system can make any kind of changes to their codes or data. This creates a safe and secure system free from tampering and fraud.

> They are free from the possibility of any kind of censorship or corruption. This is because they

are built within a network that is embedded in the principle of consensus.

➤ They are very secure against hacks, as they are based on the principles of cryptography and have no central leader that can corrupted. It is extremely difficult for a hacker to break the cryptography code.

➤ The apps can't be switched off at any time, which means there is no down-time nor can they have an error and fail.

➤ It's not necessary to integrate payment methods such as PayPal into the app to accept money transfers. As it runs on Ethereum, Ether can be used for exchanges which could be later traded for other currencies.

➤ It creates trust between the app and its users as users can see the code. Both the front-end code and back-end logic can be inspected and seen by anyone. This allows users to check and verify for themselves the security and how robust the coding is.

Here are some of the drawbacks of decentralized applications:

➤ They are built on smart contracts that depend on human capability. This means there is a margin for human error when they are initially put onto the blockchain. Bugs in the code, for example, could happen if the contract is poorly coded and can lead to unintended and adverse actions taking place. These issues are hard to control and change.

➢ This leaves open the possibility that a mistake in the code could be exploited by an attacker. The only way of stopping this is to rewrite that specific code, which requires network consensus. However, this doesn't fit the blockchain principles of being immutable. It also creates the possibility of a centralized party intervention, which goes against the essence of the blockchain's decentralized nature.

Despite its extremely safe nature, Ethereum and DAOs are not perfect. This is evident in the case of "The DAO" hack that threw a huge wrench in the works and changed Ethereum from what it was then to what it is now.

In 2016, a start-up company was working on creating a new decentralized autonomous organization that they called The DAO. The issue occurred when this specific project got hacked.

The start-up was called Slock.it and they had gathered together a team to develop venture capital firm that would allow investment decisions to be made through smart contracts rather than through human intervention. It was funded by thousands of different people through a token sale. In the end, about $150 million was raised to fund the development of the project.

However, there was a technical flaw in The DAO's software – not within the Ethereum platform, but within the smart contract – that created room for a hacker to corrupt the code and steal around $50 million worth of Ether. The fault lay with the developers of The DAO and not with Ethereum. However, the sum of money that was stolen was a significant amount and required the founders of Ethereum to get involved.

Whatever decision that the Ethereum founders made, it would have to be confirmed and agreed upon by the entire network, as a network consensus is what keeps the system decentralized and built on trust. Eventually, the community made the decision to get back the stolen funds. So, how did they manage to get back the stolen funds on a system where transactions are irreversible?

They created a hard fork, or in other words, a change in code. This works by channelling the stolen money into a different smart contract. The smart contract was coded to automatically inform the original owners when the funds were there and allow them to withdraw their specific funds.

Although the owners managed to get their money back, this process was massively controversial and became the subject of debate. This is because, as mentioned before, blockchain technology means that transactions are irreversible. Creating a hard fork went against these rules and undermined the value of the blockchain. Most importantly, it broke the idea that the blockchain is decentralized, as by creating a hard fork, this puts a central authority into the mix. Not everyone agreed with this decision, and it became a source of conflict in the Ethereum community.

This eventually created a split in the community that resulted in a new blockchain being created. The minority, who strongly disagreed with creating changes to the blockchain, even when it's in the case of rectifying hacking attacks, split from Ethereum to create Ethereum Classic, a parallel blockchain to Ethereum. The majority of the community, who supported the decision to create a hard fork to get the invested funds back, remained with Ethereum.

This is why today there exist two blockchains – Ethereum and Ethereum Classic. Their blockchains remain the same until the point where the hard fork was created. All the transactions that took place on Ethereum until the change in code are still valid and are recorded on the Ethereum Classic blockchain. It's only from the point where the hard fork was implemented that the two blockchains operate differently and separately.

This case serves to show that it is important for DAO developers to make sure that smart contracts are flawlessly constructed to avoid faults or gaps in the code where a hacker can access and manipulate the system.

Despite this split, the two seem to live quite harmoniously in the cryptocurrency world. Each one has its own group of loyal followers and each currency has seen significant increases. Despite Ethereum Classic's success, Ethereum still remains the network that most people seek to invest in.

# Chapter Summary

In this chapter, we looked at some key aspects of Ethereum. These are smart contracts, Dapps, and DAOs. They play an important role in making Ethereum a unique and valuable technology.

- Smart contracts are one of the, if not the, most important features of Ethereum. This is because they are the digital contracts that allow the diversity of applications that makes Ethereum so highly regarded. They make the potential of having different apps a reality.

- Dapps are decentralized applications. They are designed to serve a specific purpose, such as exchanging a payment or expressing the conditions of a contract. They are also being used to create exciting projects such as providing financial support to small businesses in Africa and creating interactive games similar to Minecraft.

- DAOs are Decentralized Autonomous Organizations. These are organizations that run on the blockchain and don't have any centralized leader or authority point.

- The creation of the two Ethereums – Ethereum and Ethereum Classic – was the result of a hacker successfully hacking into a flawed DAO and transferring the funds into a separate account. The majority of users agreed to make a hard fork to channel the funds back to the proper owners, but this broke the rules of the blockchain, which states that transactions are anonymous, irreversible, and most importantly, decentralized. The minority who did not agree with making this hard fork created Ethereum Classic, which is built on the same blockchain, but follows a different chain after the hard fork.

In the next chapter, we will learn more about the technology behind Ethereum and how its blockchain network works

# Chapter 3: The Technology Behind Ethereum

In this chapter, we will look at the technology behind Ethereum in more detail – namely the Ethereum Blockchain Platform and the Ethereum Virtual Machine – and also at how potential developers could go about making an application on the Ethereum blockchain.

## Ethereum Blockchain Platform

Ethereum, as we have well established, is built on blockchain technology. This means it is a digital ledger that is shared among any quantity of computers. Each time a transaction happens, it is recorded and then validated by a specific number of computers before it is released on the blockchain network. All of this is based on transparency and trust. Everyone on the network has access to the entire transaction history, so all transactions or any changes are accessible and visible to everyone.

How are transactions validated? They are validated by miners, individuals that use computers to solve complex mathematical problems to confirm a set of transactions. Each time they validate a block, they are rewarded with cryptocurrency. In the case of the Ethereum network, they earn Ether.

When someone sends funds to another person, they send it to that person's public key, which acts like a digital address. The sender uses their private key that is like a PIN to their funds and creates a transaction print. This print, or signature, as it is more commonly known, is used by miners to verify this specific transaction. Each transaction generates a new signature so that the exchange can never be repeated.

This process eliminates the need for a central authority or a third party – such as a bank – that is usually required to authorize transactions. It also removes the need to pay fees to someone to validate the transactions. This is the principle essence of blockchains. It creates a secure environment, as anything that is changed on the network has to be validated by computers. Funds are technically not really stored anywhere and are only accessible by a private key that is assigned to only one individual, making accessing someone else's funds extremely difficult.

This is the main technology of any kind of blockchain network. So, what makes Ethereum's blockchain platform special?

Ethereum uses [smart contracts, a code that the developer adds to the blockchain] They operate by performing certain activities only when certain conditions are met. This is how they follow the terms of a contract. The great thing about this is that the contract is visible to everyone. This means that any changes of the contract will be recorded, making it practically impossible to tamper with the details.

While smart contracts are not perfect, they do create exciting future possibilities. Ethereum's blockchain allows any centralized process to become decentralized, which has the potential to affect hundreds of industries, such as finance, healthcare, insurance, education, and real estate.

## Ethereum Virtual Machine

Another important part of Ethereum is the Ethereum Virtual Machine, which we looked at briefly in the last chapter. The EVM is a powerful machine known as a Turing complete 256bit Virtual Machine that allows developers to implement EVM Byte Code. In other words, anyone can use the machine to create a code.

Its key focus lies in running a secure environment for smart contracts based on the Ethereum network. It is actually isolated from the blockchain. This means a start-up or a developer looking to create a smart contract can do so on the EVM without disrupting the main blockchain network. This allows for proper testing, a vital aspect of smart contracts, as even a slightly flawed code can create huge problems. Just remember the case of The DAO project as an example.

This ability to test out technology before embedding it on the blockchain is exciting. It means that the EVM can be considered a type of learning environment that allows smart contracts to be pushed and reinvented until they are the best they can be. It creates endless possibilities for developers looking to test out new ideas without them needing to worry about affecting the blockchain.

Shifting from centralized processes to decentralized ones will be dependent on the development of smart contracts, and it is the EVM that will be play one of the biggest roles in this move.

Now you know the fundamental concepts behind Ethereum. What can you do if you want to create your own application?

Ethereum's platform allows anybody to create and implement their own apps in practically any field and for any purpose. However, despite the ease of it, it still requires developers to have a strong knowledge of network systems and coding, so a complete newbie to blockchain networks will probably have some difficulties in setting something up.

There are several ways to plug into the Ethereum network. The easiest way is to use Ethereum's own Mist browser, which has an easy-to-navigate interface and also provides a digital wallet so that users can trade and store their own

Ether. This is important, as all transactions on the Ethereum network are paid using Ethereum's cryptocurrency. [Mist is basically an access point to write, develop, and implement decentralized blockchain applications.]

Another option is to use the MetaMask browser, which is an extension that converts Google Chrome into an Ethereum browser. It allows developers to create applications from their browser. It will eventually be supported by Firefox, too. These browsers are helping to make blockchain technology accessible and bring decentralized applications into a mainstream sphere.

This will have a huge impact on the job market. As the possibilities of blockchain technology become wider and more varied, the need for blockchain developers across hundreds of industries becomes more urgent. At the moment, the demand is high, but the supply of experienced blockchain developers is low. For those considering a career change or future job prospects, studying blockchain technology may not be a bad idea at all.

## Chapter Summary

In this chapter, we looked at the technology behind Ethereum. Knowing the ins and out of the network's technology is not totally necessary to invest in Ether, but it does help you to understand its potential and have a better position in deciding whether it is a worthwhile investment or not.

- Two important parts of the Ethereum network are the Ethereum Virtual Machine and the Ethereum Blockchain Platform.

- The Ethereum Blockchain Platform is the decentralized space where Ethereum transactions take place and where new apps are created and developed.

- The Ethereum Virtual Machine is isolated from the blockchain so that developers can use it as a learning environment to test out the feasibility of new applications without damaging the blockchain.

- It is possible for almost any developer to try making their own apps for Ethereum. Developers could use Mist, Ethereum's own browser, or MetaMask, which acts as an extension of Google Chrome and turns it into an Ethereum browser.

In the next chapter, we will discover more about Ethereum mining and how it is an important part of the Ethereum network.

# Chapter 4: What Is Ethereum Mining?

In this chapter, we will look at Ethereum mining and how it works.

Blockchain technology operates on a decentralized system thanks to people who validate transactions and receive rewards for doing so. The rewards are a certain amount of cryptocurrency These validators are known as miners. Miners play a majorly important role in blockchain technology and are behind Ethereum's ability to run smoothly and transparently.

One role miners have is validating transactions in blocks and generating Ethers, meaning that the system doesn't require a central authority. Ether – Ethereum's tokens or cryptocurrency – are mined at a rate of five Ethers per mined block.

However, perhaps the most important role a miner has is to makes sure the system actually works the way it should. In traditional financial systems, banks or other institutes are the ones responsible for keeping track of all transaction records. They need to keep tabs on movement between accounts and ensure that new money isn't being created illegally. Blockchains defy convention by using a totally different way of recording transactions. They use the entire network to verify transactions instead of an intermediary. The network then adds the transactions to the public ledger for all to see. This means that every user has access to the historical record of all transactions. The whole system is dependent on a peer-to-peer community where you don't need to put all your trust and funds into the hands of one central authority.

But how do you know no one is cheating the blockchain and swindling the system?

This is where mining comes in.

Mining is the reason why decentralized record-keeping of thousands of transactions is possible. The miners work to reach a consensus on the history of each transaction. This helps prevent fraud and spending Ethers twice. As each transaction is verified through a specific signature, it makes it impossible to double spend. Ultimately, it's mining that keeps the entire network together.

How does mining actually work?

The mining process on the Ethereum platform is very similar to that of Bitcoin's platform. To process a block of transactions, miners need to use computers to calculate answers to puzzles and math equations until one of the miners gets it right. This process is quick and repeated, solving extremely complex computational math.

The process of calculation is as follows: Each block has a unique header metadata. This includes timestamp and software version. The miners pass this specific header through a hash function. By doing this, it produces a long string of numbers and letters that meets a certain fixed length. The miners change just the nonce value, which creates an impact on the hash value result.

A miner is awarded Ether when he or she matches the current target with the hash value. The block is then broadcasted across the network and the copy added to the ledger. Another miner working on that specific block will stop working on it and repeat the process on the next block.

Cheating this process is practically impossible. There is no way to pretend that work has taken place when it hasn't and there is no way of pretending to have calculated the answer to the puzzle if the miner hasn't actually answered it. The name of this type of work is known as a proof-of-work protocol.

The puzzles are controlled by algorithms. If miners start solving the puzzles quicker or slower than 12 to 15 seconds, the algorithms automatically readjust the difficulty of the equation so that the solution time remains around 15 seconds.

Each time a block is solved, the miner earns some Ether. The profitability of this depends largely on two factors: the total computing power the miners devote to solving the problems, and pure luck.

When mining for Bitcoin, the only really profitable way of mining is to use ASICs, a specialized type of mining chip that is incredibly expensive. However, for now, ASICs are not available to mine Ethereum, which can only be mined using a specific proof-of-work algorithm known as ethash.

For now, Ethereum operates its mining using a proof-of-work system. However, it plans in the future to move to proof-of-stake, which requires a different approach. The proof of stake secures the network by using owners of Ether and uses fewer resources than proof-of-work. This change will mean that the network becomes fully virtual and becomes far less energy-intensive. It will also impact Ethereum in terms of Ether value, as the demand for Ether should continue and the supply of the coin will slow down, causing a positive rise in value. For now, the date for this change is speculative, but it has been suggested it will be at the end of 2017.

## Chapter Summary

This chapter looked at mining on the Ethereum network and how it compares to mining on the Bitcoin network.

- Mining is an important part of blockchain technology, as it is what keeps the system functioning and capable of being truly decentralized.

- Mining on Ethereum uses a proof-of-work protocol. There is no way to cheat this system, as it isn't possible to fake an answer to the math equation nor is it possible to pretend to have worked if a miner hasn't. It's a tight, secure system.

- Miners, those who validate the blocks, receive Ether as rewards for their efforts. They receive five Ether per block mined. Those who help to contribute to solving a block will receive an uncle reward, which is about two or three Ethers.

- At the moment, Ethereum operates on a proof-of-work system, but this is set to change soon to a proof-of-stake system. It is thought that this change will happen at the end of 2017 and will be a gradual process that initially combines both proof of work and proof of stake until the proof of work is gradually phased out.

In the next chapter, we will look at the different uses of Ethereum and give some examples of how it's being used and its future possibilities. The next chapter should give you a better understanding of the scale of diversity that Ethereum is providing and can offer in the future. We will see why the Ethereum blockchain is so much more than just a digital payment system.

# Chapter 5: Uses Of Ethereum

In this chapter, we will take a look at the different uses of Ethereum and some examples of how it is being used.

As we have discovered in the past chapters, the Ethereum platform has become an area for potentially endless different applications across hundreds of different services and industries. The area is still new, so although application development is exciting, it is difficult to assess what will work in the long-term. However, the potential is there and the possibility for revolutionary apps is a very real possibility.

## Current Ethereum Applications

Here are some applications that are running at the moment on the Ethereum network.

➤ **BlockApps.** This is a fully comprehensive app to develop blockchain applications whether private, semi-private, or public industry specific. It helps provide the easiest ways to write, develop, and implement applications, starting from the proof of concept to production and then finally, integrating it onto the blockchain.

➤ **Weifund.** Using smart contracts, this application provides an open platform for crowdfunding. Contributions are converted into digital assets that are stored on the Ethereum blockchain and can be used, traded, and sold. It helps cut out the fees that traditional online crowdfunding platforms take from contributions.

➤ **Uport.** This application is perfect for anyone concerned about their personal identities being on a public domain. It provides a way to securely control access to personal data and can limit who can and cannot see it. By having total control, users don't need to depend on intuitions to take care of their identities and don't need to be concerned about those central institutions giving third parties their personal information.

➤ **Provenance.** This application helps to make supply chains completely transparent. The entire process is available on the blockchain, including the origin of the product. Consumers can access this app and make an informed decision about what they are buying before making the purchase.

> **Augur.** On this prediction market application, users can reap rewards by making predictions on events. Anyone can enter and make predictions, such as the winners of political elections, and those that make correct forecasts win monetary rewards. It also allows users to create their own prediction markets that ask questions about anything.

These apps have already been developed and are currently operating on the Ethereum network. You can search for them online and register to use them.

Now, let's take a step back and look at some more general uses of the Ethereum network.

We know that Ethereum is a type of blockchain technology that has the capability to support smart contracts, and as a result, support all kinds of decentralized applications that can change the way we consider traditional systems and processes. All of these uses totally cut out the intermediary. These apps can be used in hundreds of different services, effectively disrupting the traditional models of centralization. The threat remains small due to the infancy of the blockchain technology, but it is a very real possibility for the future.

Here are some areas where the Ethereum network applications can have a major impact and where applications are currently operating.

## Payment Systems

Most people associate blockchain technology with payment systems. The Bitcoin blockchain uses its network primarily for payment and Ethereum also uses its network as a payment system, among other things. While Bitcoin is still the number one cryptocurrency both in terms of popularity and value, Ether is recognized as a player on the market and is being used to pay for transactions and for exchanges on the Ethereum blockchain. Just like on the Bitcoin blockchain, miners are used to validate the transactions. The great thing about using blockchain for payments is that it makes them more secure, cheaper, as there are no intermediary fees, and anonymous for those that want more privacy.

## Investing In Gold

Not everyone would associate Ethereum with investing in gold, but that is exactly one of its uses. Using a process developed by Digix, users can use tokens to buy gold on the Ethereum blockchain. How does this work? Using the Digix app, you can exchange either Ether or fiat currency (real-life money) with gold tokens. This gold is linked to the Singaporean gold vault through a complex crypto-code. Whenever the user wants, they can switch their gold tokens for actual pieces of gold without needing to go through an intermediary or paying any large fees. This also opens up the possibility of creating similar processes for all sorts of commodities.

## Crowdfunding

What is crowdfunding? Put simply, it is when a start-up proposes an idea and broadcasts it to the world while asking for a certain amount of funds to put the idea in motion. People can donate if they want and as little or as much as they like. There are many online crowdfunding platforms. They make money by keeping a certain amount of the overall funds depending on the success of the campaign. The rest of the money then goes to the start-up. However, by using the Ethereum blockchain, the start-up can create a campaign through the network, which will be much cheaper, as any fees will simply be the fees to make the Ethereum network run. The smart contract in which the campaign is embedded will automatically send the full amount of the donations to the start-up after a successful campaign.

## Corporate Finance

As we learned earlier, The DAO was an app that allowed investors to make decisions about capital funds without any need for a middleman. Although there was a bug in The DAO platform that caused it to get hacked, the Ethereum blockchain was not to blame and still offers the capability of supporting a successful The DAO app. What is so particularly remarkable about The DAO is that it is completely unprecedented and is the possible beginning of a total change of regulatory body policies. This leaves the potential for capital fund companies being run by blockchain codes in the future rather than requiring the control of any kind of board of directors or CEO. However, the legal side of this is still very much unknown and has yet to be figured out. Still, it provides some exciting clues of what may be the future of capital investments.

Next, let's take a look at what is currently being developed for the Ethereum network.

## The Internet of Things

First of all, what is the Internet of Things? The Internet of Things is the link between the internet and everyday objects that allows them to send and receive digital information and data. Its potential is huge and some say it could become a multi-trillion-dollar market. One start-up called Slock.it is attempting to tap into this potential by developing an app on the Ethereum blockchain that links physical assets, such as apartments, bikes, or vans, to a smart contract that allows users to rent the item out. The application is called Ethereum Computer and could potentially eliminate fees to rent the assets of others. It is a kind of blockchain version of Airbnb and creates a much cheaper option for both affiliates and users.

# Casinos, Lotteries, And Online Gambling

An app on the Ethereum blockchain could allow playing the lottery or playing online poker without needing to pay fees to the giants of the gambling industries and without any concern for cheating. It will create a safe and cheaper environment for people wanting to participate in online gambling.

# Prediction Markets

As we already briefly touched on, the Ethereum blockchain provides the opportunity for prediction markets. This allows users to make bets and speculations on the outcomes of future events. The main hurdle of making this a reality at the moment is getting the information of the event from the outside world and plugging it into the blockchain in a way that is reliable.

However, some markets are already running on the Ethereum blockchain. Augur is a prediction market that is decentralized and a tool to forecast real world events. Users have the option to make predictions of happenings around the world in real time and make profit if their forecasts are correct. Augur uses the consensus of the crowd to help users make better-informed and more accurate predictions, rather like investors putting money on the stock exchange. This level of accuracy is embedded in the concept of "The

Wisdom of the Crowd." The law of this is that a group prediction is, on average, superior to those made by any one individual.

# Web Hosting

Web hosting on the Ethereum platform means that a website is hosted by everyone at the same time and supported by the blockchain, removing the chance of getting hacked or censored. Of course, the issue with this is that it creates the path for the internet to be totally free of any type of regulation, as it would become incredibly difficult for any government to take down offending sites. This could promote the development of Dark Web sites that are a thriving ground for criminal activity.

# Stablecoins

The ground is currently being laid to set the way for a new type of currency – the stablecoin. What is the stablecoin? The stablecoin is an asset that typically features price stability. Cryptocurrency is notoriously unstable, with volatile prices that are often difficult to predict. The advantage of them is that they give the user total control over their holdings. On the other hand, the US dollar is a great example of a fiat stablecoin, as it offers low volatility and so provides a reliable unit of money to invest in both the short term and the long term. However, the US dollar doesn't give the user any form of control, as it is monitored by the Federal Reserve Bank and is dependent on the banking network in the US for commercial use. To get a combination of the two – full user control and reduced volatility – is an exciting prospect. Maker is a company that is currently working on a project to make this happen by creating a currency known as the Dai, which is set to become a stablecoin that combines user control with price stability.

# Social Networks

Censorship on social media is common, especially on forums. Some companies are working to create a type of decentralized online community that operates on an open source code. This means that it will be built on smart contracts that will eliminate censorship. Whether this is good or bad is subjective, but it serves to show the diversity of smart contracts and blockchain applications.

One example of an Ethereum-based social network is Akasha. Akasha lets users publish, share, and vote for work that has been published on its platform. It aims to provide a decentralized option that gives an alternative to services such as Medium and WordPress. The system works by giving monetary incentives in the form of Ether to users to encourage engaging and rich content.

## Insurance

Insurance is expected to be revolutionized thanks to blockchain technology. The technology can streamline the user experience by using smart contracts that can automate policies depending on the customer's circumstances. It means that insurance claims could be made through the blockchain without the need for talking with an intermediary.

One app known as Dyanmis uses the blockchain to manage supplementary unemployment insurance. Based on peer-to-peer technology, it uses the social media network, LinkedIn, to help confirm the identity and employment status of its customers. Another such app is Inchain, which is a decentralized insurance platform that reduces the associated risks of losses of crypto-assets in the event of cyber-attacks or online hacking.

## ConsenSys

This app studio is a creation from Joseph Lubin, the co-founder of Ethereum. The app is a portal of products for developers, allowing them to have the correct tools to help them build apps for the Ethereum blockchain. It enables new service and business models to be constructed on the blockchain.

# Entertainment

The blockchain provides a solution to typical problems in the world of music, media, and entertainment, such as copyright issues, tracking, and payments. Two companies that are attempting to decentralize the music industry are Ujo and Peertracks. They use the Ethereum blockchain and a series of smart contracts to give artists total creative control over their work. This avoids the overhead costs associated with music platforms such as Spotify and Soundcloud. By using smart contracts, content can be distributed and managed in a way that allows artists and creators to monetize and protect their music.

Yet it's not just music that is finding its way onto the Ethereum blockchain; games are finding their footing, too. One example is the Beyond the Void app that is a real-time strategy space game that uses smart contracts to let users play an action-packed game where players need to conquer and destroy various planets and universes. There is also a decentralized eSports platform called Firstblood that lets eSports users fund and challenge each other in order to win rewards. Etherplay is an arcade-style game that runs on the Ethereum blockchain and lets users compete against each other to get top scores and win resulting rewards. VDice lets developers monetize the gambling games they create for Android Play and iOS marketplaces. The app famously made over one million dollars in around 90 minutes.

# Real Estate

The blockchain provides a platform for creating rental agreements using smart contracts on the blockchain. The smart contracts automatically fulfill their requirements when all conditions are met, such as monthly payments or deposits. It facilitates the rental process and cuts out the fees from using lawyers and middlemen. This is also a possibility for mortgages and loans. It also lets people list and search for properties without any fees from a real estate intermediary.

# Energy Transfer

TransActive Grid is a great app for promoting environmentally-conscious practices. It is the result of a collaboration between Siemens and LO3 energy. It allows residents of a particular area to either transfer or sell the excess renewable energy that they have stored to their neighbors. The exchange is done automatically and provides a cheap and highly efficient way for energy transfer within communities and areas that use solar panels. At the moment, it is currently running in Brooklyn, New York.

Other examples include ElectricChain, which is using Ethereum blockchain technology to work with solar energy partners to help encourage more people to use solar energy.

# Marriage Contracts And Wills

At the moment, there is no legal precedent for this, so the viability of these documents in court is untested. However, the possibility is being considered for writing marriage contracts or wills and encoding them on the blockchain. It could be a good place to store paper contracts digitally in case the original is lost.

# Decentralized Cryptocurrency Exchange

A decentralized cryptocurrency exchange is a possibility. Right now, the EtherEx is in development for an exchange that operates on the blockchain and is available for cryptocurrencies. It means that all exchanges would take place virtually without any central leader or person controlling the movement of currency.

# Supply Chain Management

Using the blockchain to create a series of smart contracts to help manage the supply chain could provide an effective tool for streamlining and facilitating the process. All the steps of the process can be embedded into the blockchain, which would make the process quicker more efficient.

The Ethereum blockchain is being used for all of the aforementioned purposes. Now, let's take a look at some possible uses for the future. These are not currently feasible just yet, as more time and consideration is required, but there are some apps that are testing the waters of these possibilities. It hints at the diverse potential of the Ethereum blockchain.

# Financial Markets

Using the blockchain for financial markets would mark the end of fraud and market manipulation. However, the key obstacle here is creating a financial market that the banks and governments would approve of, which would be extremely difficult. The financial markets rake in enormous profits for those in power. By moving the market onto a public blockchain, all those profits would be wiped out. A more feasible option would be moving the financial markets onto a private blockchain with more regulation.

However, that isn't to say that apps are not being developed. The Branche platform provides solutions to financial services, such as check cashing and credit assessment using the Ethereum blockchain. ICONOMI is a decentralized platform that give investors a range of financial tools to help return high profits on a decentralized economy.

## Elections And Votes

Having voting take place on the blockchain would create fair and secure elections, ensuring everyone gets a vote and there is no tampering or rigging involved.

The potential for using blockchain technology is huge. The number of blockchain apps currently available continues to grow as more developers create new and better apps. The global blockchain market value was calculated at around $120.2 million in 2016. This is expected to grow to $2.3 billion by 2021. This is extraordinary growth for such a young technology network.

This growth is largely thanks to smart contracts on the Ethereum blockchain that can provide opportunities for thousands of innovative and exciting new uses. Its potential to revolutionize industries is huge and the idea of it becoming a mainstream technology isn't far-fetched at all.

## Chapter Summary

In this chapter, we looked at the different uses of Ethereum. By now, you should understand the enormous potential Ethereum has and why it is currently the most exciting and revolutionary of the blockchain technologies.

- Some apps are already in operation that provide varied services from data protection to changing the way the supply process works.

- Some near-future uses include payment systems, investing in gold, corporate finance, and crowdfunding.

- Other future potential uses include insurance exchanges, web hosting, social networks, entertainment and gambling, real estate contracts, and election voting.

In the next chapter, we will look at Ether, Ethereum's currency.

# Chapter 6: What Is Ether?

In this chapter, we will look at Ether, Ethereum's associated cryptocurrency.

As we know, Ethereum is a decentralized blockchain that has the capability to write smart contracts on its platform and ultimately create potentially thousands of different applications that can revolutionize industries and centralized systems.

However, although Ethereum is a kind of decentralized system, it is not exactly free. To make transactions, to mine blocks, and to support services, some kind of exchange is required. This exchange is done with a particular, special code that can reward miners for their efforts to validate blocks and pay for the computational resources that are required to run applications. This code is known as Ether.

Similar to the globally famous Bitcoin, Ether is an asset that exists digitally. However, rather than thinking of it as a cryptocurrency or a form of payment, it is more accurate to see Ether as a way to fuel and support the decentralized applications that exist on the Ethereum network. For example, the transaction fees of Ethereum are calculated according to how much energy the action requires, which is based on computational power and the time it takes to run.

Unlike Bitcoin, which has a strong economic structure and a hard cap of 21 million bitcoins, Ether's structure is far looser and open-ended. There is no cap limit. In terms of quantity of Ether, the amount is technically endless.

In a 2014 crowdfunding campaign, 60 million Ether were purchased by users. Later, another 12 million went to the Ethereum Foundation. This group is a collection of researchers and developers that help to develop and improve the technology that sits at the foundations of Ethereum.

In addition to these quantities, five Ethers are assigned to the miners that validate the transactions on the network through blocks every 12 seconds. It is calculated that at the most, 18 million Ether are mined each year. Also, those that help solve a block puzzle receive what is known as an uncle reward. This is the equivalent of about two or three Ethers.

This means that the total number of Ether is not really known nor is the pace of Ether creation. One thing that is certain, though, is that the price of Ether is going up as its value continues to increase month by month.

This increase has caught the attention of both potential investors and critics. Many wonder how the price will act in the future and this question has proved difficult to predict.

Some experts believe that Ether could overtake Bitcoin in terms of value, while others warn that the price of Ether is simply the result of an inflated demand and could suddenly drop.

## What Factors Affect Ether's Price?

One of the most important factors that influences the price of Ether is ICOs or Initial Coin Offerings. This is the platform that allows investors to exchange Ether for different digital tokens.

These offerings have had a huge impact on the value of Ether. The reason is that some of the offerings have been able to generate millions of dollars worth of tokens in minutes, which has captured interest and increased their visibility.

Other factors that affect the price of Ether include:

> ➢ The development of new apps on the Ethereum blockchain. Ethereum is so much more than simply a digital asset. It was never created to compete against altcoins, but to be something totally unique and different. The more apps that are created and adopted using Ethereum's blockchain technology, the higher the demand will be for Ether. The higher the demand, the higher the price.

> ➤ Media coverage has an effect on Ether prices, too. The value of Ether rose by 5,000% in the first few months of 2017, which naturally caused quite a stir in the media. This kind of exposure can increase the level of adoption of Ether and increase the overall demand, driving up the price even more.

> ➤ At the moment, Ether is generated on a proof-of-work mining protocol. However, the founders of Ethereum intend to change this in the future to a proof-of-stake protocol. This means that the number of Ether produced per month will decrease. Coupled with the increase in media coverage that the change will bring, the demand and prices for Ether could increase.

> ➤ On a negative note, if any of the systems or apps are hacked or attacked, this could lower market confidence and result in a drop in Ether value.

> ➤ The price of Ether is linked to the success of Ethereum. If for any reason Ethereum fails or is not as successful as it was expected to be, then the value of Ether will crash.

Overall, Ether is the currency of Ethereum. While it is exchanged on global exchange sites, it is more a fuel to pay for services on the Ethereum blockchain than it is an altcoin. If Ethereum continues to be successful and recognized for its enormous potential and technological value, Ether will continue to be valuable.

# Chapter Summary

In this chapter, we looked at Ethereum's currency known as Ether. Sometimes the exchanges use the terms Ethereum and Ether interchangeably, because as Ether is used specifically for services on the Ethereum network, buying Ether is like investing in the Ethereum network.

- Unlike Bitcoin, which is specifically designed to be a digital currency, Ether can be seen more as a fuel to support the operations on the Ethereum network.

- Ether has no market cap and the exact number of Ether in circulation is unknown.

- A crowdfunding campaign produced the initial 60 million Ether coins in 2014.

- For every new block mined, the miner receives five Ether. The average time that it takes to mine a block is between 12 and 15 seconds. It is estimated that around 18 million Ether are mined per year.

- The value of Ether has risen dramatically over the last few months and it is expected that its value will continue to increase.

In the next chapter, we will take a look at the financial history of Ether in more detail.

# Chapter 7: The Financial History Of Ether

In this chapter, we will explore the financial history of Ether, beginning with how Ether currently looks on the market.

In terms of digital assets, the one that offers the highest value proposition is Bitcoin. It is the oldest and most popular cryptocurrency available and continues to be the most valuable.

So, what's the appeal of Bitcoin? Bitcoin is considered to be fairly volatile, but its market remains one of the most stable out of all of the cryptocurrencies. In September 2017, Bitcoin's market cap was around six and a half billion dollars.

There are hundreds of other cryptocurrencies on the market that offer value, but many of these also come with much higher volatility. Within this subset of the market is Ether, the currency of the Ethereum platform. It has experienced great recent success and is seen as a contender for investment portfolios. Ether has several key benefits that Bitcoin and other cryptocurrencies can't provide, but it comes with risks and things to consider before investing. There are also some important factors that influence the price of Ether that need to be understood.

Ether was developed to pay for actions and transactions on the Ethereum network. Users receive Ether for their efforts and energy spent in validating blocks and contributing to the development of Ethereum. This is the key difference between Ether and Bitcoin – whereas Ether has a specific, localized use, Bitcoin was designed to become a global digital currency used to pay for virtually anything.

The market that Ether operates on is interconnected with the one that Bitcoin is associated with. Many of the exchanges and infrastructure used for Bitcoin is also used for Ether. There are several exchange platforms, such as Bitfinex where users buy Bitcoin and other cryptocurrencies. Now, they can buy Ether there, too.

The market for Ether developed differently than the market for Bitcoin. Bitcoin's value grew as more and more people started to use it, especially as people could make more bitcoins through mining. Contrastingly, Ethereum made a pre-sale of Ether tokens in 2015. As a result of this launch, more than $14 million was raised from this form of informal IPO (initial public offering). It was this initial donation that created the initial supply of Ether. The initial supply was around 72 million Ether, which was split between two parties – 60 million went to the contributors to the presale and 12 million went to the Ethereum development fund. After this, Ethereum created (and continues to create) five Ether for every block mined. A total of 18 million Ether can be released on the market every year.

This makes the supply of Ether inconsistent and unknown. Bitcoin, on the other hand, has a consistent supply rate and the rules in the Bitcoin software allow only 21 million bitcoins to be in existence at a time. Currently, new Bitcoin tokens are issued at about 25 new tokens every ten minutes. This rate automatically slows down as the limit of 21 million approaches.

You may be wondering if mining affects the price. And if it does, how? In terms of Bitcoin, the price is affected by the steady release of new bitcoins to the miners that validate the blocks. This means that mining affects the price of the coin by increasing the supply of the coin. Ethereum works on a similar system. It operates on a proof-of-work algorithm so that miners receive five Ethers for every new block. On average, miners at Ethereum mine a new block every 15 seconds. Miners that assist in the solving process but do not actually solve the problem receive two or three Ethers as a reward for helping.

The value of Ether may change when Ethereum introduces Casper, a proof-of-stake protocol. It provides a smaller mining subsidy, so the rate of blocks mined per 15 seconds will most likely change.

# The Price Volatility Of Ether

Ether is still a young token, and as a result, it experiences sharp prices increases and decreases. Such volatility may seem to indicate that the currency is not a viable investment, but volatility can actually provide profitable trading opportunities. Traders can speculate on future price moves and use this to calculate when best to buy Ether (just before a rise in price) and when best to sell it (just before a dip in price).

# Ether's Historical Prices

The value of Ether has changed drastically numerous times. For a while after its introduction in 2015, the value of Ether didn't even get above $2 per Ether. Throughout 2016 and until February 2017, the value of Ether hovered around $15, fluctuating around this figure. However, the end of February 2017 saw a complete change in direction.

By June 2017, the value of Ether shot up to around $340 per Ether. Since then, the value has been quite volatile. In July 2017, the value per Ether dropped to $170. In September 2017, the value went back up to around $260 per Ether.

Something worth considering when it comes to the value of Ether is its purpose. It was never really intended to be a competing altcoin in the world of cryptocurrency.

Ethereum was developed for its multi-purpose app capability and Ether is a means to pay and support its services. Bitcoin, on the other hand, was specifically developed to be a digital currency and achieve a high value. Although it is easy and common to compare Bitcoin and Ether, their purposes are actually very different. Whether the value of Ether will continue to increase is hard to speculate, but as Ethereum continues to enjoy popularity, it is expected that Ether's value will continue to rise for in the near future.

## Chapter Summary

In this chapter, we looked at some of the key points of Ether's financial history.

- Although it was never really intended as a worldwide digital currency like Bitcoin, Ether is still being traded on global markets as traders begin to see the potential profits in it.

- When first released, the value of Ether was below $2 per Ether. 2017 saw a total change in direction when it shot up to around $340 per Ether. At the time of writing, is hovering around the $260 mark.

- As the mainstream adoption of Ethereum becomes more likely, the value of Ether will likely increase.

In the next chapter, we will look at the best ways of buying, selling, and storing Ether.

# Chapter 8: How To Buy, Sell, And Store Ether

In this chapter, we will cover the possible ways of buying, selling, and storing Ether.

Let's start by looking at how to buy Ether.

First of all, it's important to iron out a few things. Ethereum is the blockchain platform that allows developers to build apps within the network. It can be used to decentralize, code, and trade almost anything.

So, what is Ether, then?

Ether is the currency of the Ethereum platform and is needed for trading and building apps on the network. Like Bitcoin, it can be traded and mined. The confusing part is when people start using the words "Ethereum" and "Ether" interchangeably. If people mention buying Ethereum, they mean Ether.

Although often treated as a currency, the makers of Ethereum are quite clear when they say that Ether is not so much a currency as it is a crypto-fuel. In other words, it is simply a token that is used to pay for services on the Ethereum platform or to pay miners when they validate a block.

What does this mean for investors?

It means that unlike Bitcoin, you won't be able to buy things online with it. However, you can still buy it for trading and investing while implementing strategies to make profits on it if or when the price goes up.

It's worth noting that while Bitcoin is established and mature, Ether is still in its infancy. As a result, it is a great coin for experienced investors. Saying that, with some research, it is still possible for an inexperienced investor to profit by investing in Ether. Just make sure you do your homework and look for news that talks about both Ether's and Ethereum's future.

You may notice there are two types of cryptocurrencies that relate to Ethereum – Ethereum (or Ether) and Ethereum Classic. So, what's the difference?

As covered earlier, the two cryptocurrencies were once the same before a disagreement split Ethereum. The disagreement couldn't be reconciled and, as a result, Ethereum continued as two distinct blockchains – Ethereum (including the hard fork) and Ethereum Classic (without the hard fork).

This means that there are two different currencies for Ethereum that have two exchange rates. Ether's value is higher and it is more common.

## Buying Ether

Whether you want to buy Ether with a credit card, cash, or a wire transfer, there are several options available.

One of the most convenient ways of buying Ether (or Ethereum, as you will probably see it called on exchanges) is through one of the Bitcoin financial exchanges that also have supplies of Ether.

There are several Bitcoin exchanges that also sell Ether, such as shapeshift.io, Poloniex, and Kraken. However, the most popular exchanges used to buy Ether are the following:

## Coinbase

It's possible to buy Ether through Coinbase, which is one of the easiest and cheapest ways to do so. It is only available in certain countries, so it is important to check this before attempting to buy this way.

It is easy to buy from Coinbase. Simply open a Coinbase free account. Then you can add a payment method that you can keep for all transactions. This will include adding your credit card or bank account details. Next, go to the Buy/Sell section on the site and select the amount of Ether that you want to buy. Confirm your transaction by clicking "Buy Ethereum". Yes, it does say Ethereum rather than

Ether. Don't worry, in this case, it is the same thing. There is a small transaction fee, which is largely dependent on your method of payment. Credit cards always have a higher fee. The fee varies between 1.49% to 3.99%.

## Cex.io

Available in most countries across the world, Cex.io offers a crypto-exchange to a much wider audience. It is known famously as a Bitcoin exchange, but it also sells Ether. The exchange rate seems quite high when compared to other exchanges. The reason for this is that the fees are already factored in, so the price you see is the price you pay.

It's really easy to buy Ether on Cex.io. You can buy Ether using Bitcoin through a direct transfer on the site or pay in US dollars or euro. If you are using a credit card in a different currency, then you just fund your account with Cex.io from money on your card and pay that way.

## Coinmama

Having been in operation since 2014, Coinmama has become a reputable exchange and the best part about it is that it sells Ether worldwide. The site is very user-friendly and makes buying with a credit card or cash simple and convenient. When compared to other exchanges, Coinmama offers fair exchange rates.

## Coinhouse

Coinhouse is especially good for those who live in the EU. Started in France, the Bitcoin and Ether exchange platform eventually branched out to supply the rest of the EU with opportunities to buy cryptocurrency. It is relatively straightforward buying Ether on Coinhouse and they accept payments with credit card, debit card, and Neosurf.

In case you are not familiar with the term, Neosurf is a nifty alternative payment method that helps support customers that prefer not to enter their personal information online, such as bank account information or credit card details. It is effectively a prepaid voucher that users can use to make purchases online anonymously and securely.

## Can You Buy Ether With Cash?

Buying Ether with cash is a little tricky in most cases. For bitcoins, there are options such as LocalBitcoins where you can meet people and buy bitcoins with cash in person. However, this doesn't exist for Ether just yet. To buy Ether with cash, the best way of doing it is to buy bitcoins in cash and then buy Ether using the bitcoins on an online exchange.

## What About Trading Ether?

This is a good option for those that want to trade, but don't want to buy. In other words, those that are looking to profit on Ether on the exchange rate. The way to do this is to get Ethereum CFDs (Contract For Difference), which allows you to trade according to the exchange rate without actually buying Ether. This is quite risky and is best left to experienced traders that understand the exchanges well. The only place to get Ethereum CFDs at the moment is Plus500.

## Selling Ether

There are several ways to sell Ether.

One of the most popular and convenient ways of selling Ether is through the exchanges.

The way to sell on the exchanges is to deposit the funds into the exchange of your choice and then begin trading. You will need to open an account before you can deposit or withdraw any fiat money from cryptocurrency. We have already covered some of the most popular exchanges.

You can also sell your Ether over the counter – kind of. There are some places where you can exchange cryptocurrency directly for cash and do this in person. While this is not yet available for Ether, it is available for Bitcoins. One way of selling Ether here is to exchange your Ether for Bitcoins first and then take the Bitcoins to the counter to swap for cash. Just check that the counter you go to is a reputable trader, as scammers and thieves are not unheard of.

Another way of selling Ether is exchanging it for other cryptocurrencies. A great site for doing this is Shapeshift. Selling Ether for other cryptocurrencies can give you more choices on where you spend your money.

## Storing Ether

Purchasing and selling Ether is pretty straightforward and is most common on cryptocurrency exchanges such as Coinbase, Bitfinex, and Ploniex. They are also spaces to store your Ether, as they provide online wallets in which to keep cryptocurrency. Finding the best place to store you Ether is critical to avoid hackers and technical issues. As with all cryptocurrencies, if you are looking to store Ether long term, the best bet is store them in cold storage, such as on a USB stick. Whatever way you choose, you'll still probably find many options on the market. Here are some of the safest and most popular.

Coinbase is one of the best exchanges for cryptocurrency. Once you open an account on Coinbase, you will automatically get a free cryptocurrency wallet. While it certainly comes recommended for exchanging currencies, it is not necessarily the safest place to keep your Ether. Why? The fact that it is a centralized exchange that stores all the private keys in one database makes it a target for hacking. It holds millions of private keys on its database, which is the hacking equivalent of a treasure chest.

Although Coinbase has a squeaky-clean reputation so far, it pays to look at other centralized storage systems that have fallen to the hands of crafty hackers to understand the dangers of storing cryptocurrency in centralized systems. One of the most famous incidents was the Mt.Gox hack in February 2014. Prior to this date, Mt.Gox handled more than 70% of all worldwide Bitcoin transactions. However, a technical glitch meant a hacker was able to access the Bitcoin accounts, resulting in Mt.Gox suspending all trading, closing its website, and filing for bankruptcy. The hackers managed to steal around $350 million worth of Bitcoin. The worst part is that as Bitcoin transactions are irreversible (all blockchain transactions, in fact), it's practically impossible to get this money back.

For this reason, it's best to invest in a hardware wallet, especially if you are in possession of a large amount of Ether.

# Hardware Wallets

Hardware wallets are relatively simple and offer a safe and private way of storing cryptocurrencies. They are also free from the danger of getting infected by malware. Passwords and files on the computer may be safe the majority of the time, but they are susceptible to hacking. This is why it is also a good idea to split your coins between several wallets to minimize losses should you get hacked.

Let's take a look at some of the best types of hardware wallets to use. Hardware wallets are basically like specialized USB sticks.

The Ledge Nano S hardware wallet is a great option for storing Ether offline. In addition to supporting Bitcoin and a wide variety of altcoins, this hardware wallet supports Ether.

Using this wallet, you can send and receive payments, check your accounts, and manage several addresses in one space. It also contains a system that simplifies the authentication process for several compatible services, such as Dropbox and Google. The Nano S also provides a backup paper wallet as a special recovery feature. For security, it has a dual-chip architecture. When you connect this device to the computer, it uses the Google Chrome extension. You can create a four-digit pin on the device to use before connecting to the blockchain, which helps to eliminate the chance of anyone hacking the keys.

Trezor is another USB hardware wallet. It is also one of the most secure and offers several security measures for you to pick from. It was originally developed for storing Bitcoin, but more recently has been made available for supporting altcoins, including Ether. It comes heavily secured, which is great for those who are looking to invest in a slightly more expensive wallet for complete peace of mind. The security features include avoiding showing any of your PIN characters on your computer, so when you connect your device to your computer and enter your PIN, the digits appear not on the computer screen but on the USB screen, minimizing the chance of someone accessing your password.

One great advantage of Trezor is that there is a two-factor authentication for added security. This means that should you lose your Trezor, you can use a series of secret words that you have encoded to allow you to regain access to your money, account history, and keys.

## Hot Wallets

Hardware wallets, or cold storage, as they are sometimes known, tend to be considered the safest. However, there are other options, including desktop wallets, sometimes known as hot wallets. Their security is highly dependent on the level of security your computer has. The reason why hot wallets are considered less safe than cold storage is that they are always connected to the internet, making them more vulnerable to theft.

However, hot wallets such as desktop wallets or mobile phone app wallets are convenient and allow quick and easy access. This is a distinct advantage for those who trade Ether which is why hot wallets tend to be more popular among those that are looking for short-term storage options.

For a hot wallet that gives more control to its users, Exodus is a great option. It is a software application that combines the best of both worlds – it's a hot wallet, but it is also available for download on your computer. As a result, your private keys are not stored on their servers, giving you more control over the security of your account. As an independent wallet, it encrypts and stores the private keys and your transaction data on your computer rather than an external server. This means that your data isn't shared and there aren't any hackable accounts or servers.

Exodus supports Ether, as well as Bitcoin and a few other altcoins. It has a user-friendly interface and simple layout. One feature that has proved popular among its users is a simple pie-chart that is unique to each user and visually shows the user's cryptocurrency holdings. This shows the proportion of all the different types of cryptocurrency you have and gives the overall value.

Another great feature of Exodus is that users receive a backup link through their email. This means, in the case that your computer is destroyed for whatever reason, you can use the backup link and install it on another machine.

Exodus also lets you convert between cryptocurrencies without leaving the application or depositing into an exchange. ShapeShift.io is a crypto-asset exchange and is integrated into Exodus, allowing exchanges to take place on the same platform.

In terms of storing, then, it's the cold storage wallets – such as USB wallets – that tend to be the most secure. However, if you are a regular trader, then you may prefer getting a desktop wallet or mobile wallet for your smartphone. Out of the two, the app for the smart phone tends to be safer than the one for the desktop, as it is less prone to viruses. Although the wallets that come free with the exchanges are tempting to use and tend to be safe, their appeal to hackers is high and carries this related risk. It is advisable not to use these wallets.

## Chapter Summary

In this chapter, we looked at the different ways of buying, selling, and storing your Ether.

- There are three options for buying Ether. The most common is to buy on the exchanges with fiat money. Another way of buying Ether is to buy with cash, but this has to be done indirectly by first buying Bitcoin with Ether and then swapping for cash. Finally, Ether can be traded for other cryptocurrencies on the exchanges.

- Selling Ether follows the same rules as buying Ether. You can sell on the exchanges for fiat money, sell in cash by first exchanging it for Bitcoin, or sell for other cryptocurrencies.

- Storing Ether is extremely important. If you are looking for a long-term investment in Ether, then you should consider cold storage, which is a hardware wallet that is effectively a specialized USB stick. This is the most secure out of the storage options. If you are a trader, you may consider a desktop wallet or smartphone app, as it is far more convenient to make transactions quickly than it is with a hardware wallet. It is not recommended to use an online wallet through a third party, as this takes away some of your control over your funds and presents a tempting target for hackers.

In the next chapter, we will look at how you can mine for Ether. Mining is one of the most important and consistent ways of generating new Ether.

# Chapter 9: Nine: The Mining Process Of Ether

In this chapter, we will take a look at the mining process of Ether. A common question regarding Ether, from people who are familiar with Bitcoin, is if you can earn Ether through mining.

The answer is: yes, you can earn Ether by mining. Similar to the mining of Bitcoin, Ethereum uses a protocol known as "proof of work" that lets miners validate blocks and receive a reward for every block they mine.

It is possible to mine Ether on your own computer, which is known as CPU mining. However, it is hard and you probably won't get the rewards you are looking for. Nowadays, it is hard to make any kind of profit using a CPU. The best way of earning a reasonable and worthwhile quantity of Ether is to have a dedicated GPU set up that is specifically created for the job of mining. GPUs are much faster than CPUs, which makes them a more profitable resource to use when mining. When you consider that even the simplest and most basic of GPUs is 200 times faster than a CPU, it makes sense to invest in a GPU rather than attempt to mine using a CPU.

Let's take a look at how you can mine for Ether.

Ethereum mining is relatively easy. There is no requirement to download the entire Ethereum blockchain (which is extremely helpful when you realize that the blockchain is now over 20 GBs and will keep growing).

One of the most popular setups for mining Ether is using the Claymore Miner. It's an easy process that involves getting a wallet, downloading the miner, configuring it to Windows, and then finally getting your batch file to run. The overall process takes less than 10 minutes, and then you are ready to start mining.

One concern about mining for cryptocurrency is that it uses a lot of energy, so your electricity bill can be high afterward. However, if you mine Ether correctly and then sell it, this should cover the costs of the electricity that was required to mine and give you a profit, too!

Another common consideration is whether to solo mine or pool mine. Solo mining is when you work alone to generate Ether. Pool mining is when you work together with a group of miners. This group shares the processing power and splits their rewards equally or according to the time contribution from each miner. Pool mining tends to be the most profitable. It is hard to mine alone, unless you have the latest, biggest, and most expensive mining hardware. Pool mining generates a steady earning and you can earn both through solving puzzles for blocks and for contributing.

So what equipment do you need to mine? Besides the GPU, there are a few other things you will need:

> You will want to make sure your Windows 10 OS is a 64-bit installation.

> It is important that you have a motherboard with a sufficient number of PCI-E slots to easily support all the cards that you will be running.

> A powered PCI-E riser is important for each extra GPU that you have (if you are using more than one).

> Another important thing to consider if you are using more than one GPU is that your PSU has enough connections to support all the GPUs that you are using.

> You will need a basic CPU with at least 4GB of RAM. It is also important to make sure that your CPU, the motherboard, and the RAM are all compatible.

> It seems an obvious thing, but it can get overlooked – you need a power button so that you can turn the system on and off.

> You will also need a monitor, a mouse, and a basic keyboard.

When it comes to mining, sometimes there are other mining options, such as using ASIC hardware, gaming laptops, and virtual environments.

When it comes to Ether, you can mine it simply by having a system that meets the points above and one GPU (or more, if you like) with at least 3GB of RAM. But, how about the other options? Are they worth using for Ether?

ASICs are great for some cryptocurrencies, such as Bitcoin and Dash, but there are no ASICs for Ethereum. It is better to use Mining Rigs for Ethereum, as it is still profitable.

Gaming laptops do actually have high-end cards. However, mining generates high levels of energy (or in other words, high levels of heat), which can damage your laptop, so in this case it is better to have a desktop.

Virtual environments tend not to be that profitable as they don't have enough powerful GPU in them.

Sticking to the requirements above and using a GPU is the best way to mine Ether and make profits.

## Why Mine Ethereum?

There are several great reasons to mine Ether:

> ➤ If you buy a GPU, mining is a good way to help fund its cost. A GPU can be quite expensive, so

mining provides a chance to pay back the cost and then making a profit.

➢ Mining Ether is a great way to build up a savings of tokens and then trade them for bitcoins. This provides a way of getting a cheaper entry into the world of Bitcoin.

➢ Alternatively, you can buy bitcoins and then exchange them for cash. So, mining for Ether is way of earning cash.

➢ If you're a trader, then mining for Ether can be a great way of getting on board with the volatile Ethereum markets. Depending on your experience, skill, and sometimes just pure luck, you can trade your Ether rewards to make a good profit.

# How Do I Start Mining?

As we have looked at in this book, blockchains in cryptocurrency are made up of blocks. Blocks are technically batches of transactions and in Ethereum they occur around every 15 seconds. The mining process serves to validate and record these blocks. Let's take a look at how this works in more detail:

➢ Mining begins with the miners collecting all the transactions they feel are valid from the network. What criteria confirm validity? This is usually judged in terms of code, fees, and the accounting history. The miners gather these transactions and put them into blocks.

➤ Miners then hash the block with the GPUs, which is an energy-intensive process. For each successful hash result, a proof of work is produced that proves that a particular miner has worked on that certain block.

➤ The rest of the network needs to confirm and accept that this block is valid. If they do, then the block becomes part of the blockchain and is permanently there.

➤ Once the block has gone onto the blockchain, the miner will receive five Ether, as well as all the transaction and code processing fees within their block.

All cryptocurrencies exist on a blockchain. As Bitcoin is the most common and the one most people know about, we can use it to compare to Ethereum. So, how does the blockchain for Bitcoin compare to Ethereum's blockchain?

The main difference is the hashing algorithm. This is why the special hashing hardware, known as ASICs, used in Bitcoin mining is not compatible with Ethereum, and hence why ASICs can't be used to mine Ether. The name of Ethereum's algorithm is Ethash and it's a memory-hard algorithm. This means it has been created so that it can't be used with ASICs and its structure is not suitable for an Ethereum-mining ASIC. The best way to mine Ether is by using a GPU.

Mining for Ethereum is kept at a steady 15 seconds. This means that it takes about 15 seconds to mine each block. Surely though, with practice, the speed of solving a block would become quicker? The answer is no. To solve a block, the computer needs to solve complex equations. To ensure that the interval to solve a block stays around 15 seconds, the level of difficulty is increased to ensure that it can't be solved any quicker. If it gets too difficult and it takes too long to solve the equation, the level of difficulty is adjusted to an easier level. These adjustments constantly take place to maintain a 15 second average.

This is the process of mining and Ether creation. For now, mining works through the proof-of-work protocol, but this is set to change soon to the proof-of-stake protocol. Mining will still take place initially, as it will take some time to totally phase out the proof-of-work set up. Eventually, though, mining for Ether will cease to exist.

## Chapter Summary

In this chapter, we looked at everything you need to know about mining for Ether.

- You can earn Ether through mining. It is easier (and cheaper) to earn Ether by mining the Ethereum blockchain than it is to earn bitcoins by mining the Bitcoin blockchain.

- Mining with a CPU is not the most effective way of mining Ether – you need a GPU. Ignore any ads for ASICs for Ether, as no ASICs will work for the Ethereum network.

- At the moment, Ethereum works on a proof-of-work protocol, but in the future, it will change to a proof-of-stake system. While this change will be gradual, once fully implemented, mining for Ether will no longer be possible.

In the next chapter, we will look at the factors to consider when deciding whether to invest in Ether or not. We will look at both the pros and cons so you can decide for yourself whether it is a good investment for you.

# Chapter 10: Should I Invest In Ether?

In this chapter, we will take a look at the pros and cons of investing in Ether. I believe that Ether makes a good investment, especially now that Ethereum is becoming increasingly well-known and its development looks highly promising. However, I will present all the advantages and drawbacks for investing in Ether so you can decide for yourself if it would make a good investment and addition to your portfolio.

Although we've already covered that Ether's value has risen considerably in 2017, it bears mentioning again here. From the beginning of the year to the middle of 2017, the value of Ether rose by almost 5,000%. Despite critics predicting an impending crash, this seems unlikely, as the value of most cryptocurrencies continues to rise or at least remain stable. For those that are experiencing price drops, they are minor dips rather than plummeting crashes. Investing in cryptocurrencies right now – and this includes Ether – can still be a profitable move.

A natural concern many investors have about Ether is that it gave such huge returns in such a short period of time. – we're talking about that 5,000% increase in value in six months. This kind of investment seems too good to be true and will automatically set off alarm bells for seasoned investors.

However, Ether is no ordinary investment and growth like this is perfectly feasible. Ethereum is totally different from other technologies. Although it operates using blockchain technology, it is the first of its kind that so easily supports not just a digital payment system, but a platform for thousands of decentralized apps. It has the potential to completely disrupt hundreds of industries and services as we know them, turning centralized processes into decentralized ones. It is set to potentially revolutionize the way we manage finances, the internet, and business.

For this reason, Ethereum doesn't seem likely to be going anywhere any time soon. It has a high chance of mainstream adoption and, as a result, it is seemingly safe to invest in its cryptocurrency. It is expected that Ether will overtake Bitcoin as the largest cryptocurrency on the market by market cap. If (more likely, when) this happens, the media coverage of Ethereum and Ether will be huge, leading to a further increase in price that will put it way ahead of Bitcoin.

It's worth remembering that Ethereum is more than just a cryptocurrency and that it is an open source network that is far superior technically than any other blockchain. The names Ethereum and Ether are often used interchangeably and there is a good reason for that. When you buy

Ethereum, you are in fact buying Ether, which is the currency that supports the network. So, when you buy Ether, you are investing in the network. You are channelling your money into the network, the most powerful and diverse blockchain in existence. Its potential is endless and in terms of investment, these facts about Ethereum make it highly attractive.

So why should you invest in Ethereum?

First of all, Ethereum has more applications than Bitcoin.

Cryptocurrencies are great for their fast, effective, and safe features. The novelty of a currency that is immune to hyperinflation and that is not controlled by a central authority is highly appealing. However, the most exciting part of the cryptocurrency world is the technology that supports it – the blockchain network.

Ethereum's blockchain is way more advanced than Bitcoin's. What gives it the ability to support more apps than Bitcoin is that it is written in Turing-complete code language, which means that it is capable of running any algorithm. In other words, any script can run on Ethereum, allowing developers to create almost anything. Ethereum is also a whole lot faster than Bitcoin, processing its blocks in an average of 15 seconds compared to Bitcoin's 20 minutes. These features make Ethereum the best network by far.

Another reason to invest in Ethereum is that it is supported by several Fortune 500 companies, which credits its potential and value. A group called the EEA (Enterprise Ethereum Alliance) includes a set of powerful companies –

among them J.P. Morgan, Microsoft, and Intel – that created this collaboration to develop the Ethereum technology in order to incorporate it into their systems in the future. The appeal lies in its efficiency, its speed, and also the flexibility that smart contracts bring.

These features bring us to the final reason to invest in Ethereum. Financial institutions are beginning to use it.

If any cryptocurrency is likely to adopted in mass, then it would be Ether. Banking systems can work with Ethereum thanks to the smart contracts. Bitcoin, on the other hand, would completely disrupt the banking system as we know it, which means banks and central authorities are reluctant to use it. However, some banks are willingly adopting Ethereum-based systems, such as using the app to help customers make securer transactions. Financial institutions see Bitcoin as a possible threat, but they see Ethereum as a way to streamline their services and bring better experiences to their customers.

From an investor's point of view, these are some key reasons to consider investing in Ethereum.

There are still more reasons that Ethereum is a good potential investment. Here are a few:

> It is safe. Ethereum is an extremely safe platform and smart contracts are practically unbreakable. There are plenty of features that prevent abuse of the network and its high level of coding means that hacking the system is incredibly difficult, if not impossible.

➤ The price of Ether is relatively stable at the moment. While Ethereum did suffer a hacking incident (The DAO case) and the split involving the hard fork, the blockchain was hardly affected and the technology remains in demand.

➤ The team behind Ethereum is incredibly skilled. The programmer that created Ethereum was Vitalik Buterin, a former bronze medal holder at the International Olympiads in Informatics at the age of 17. In 2012, he co-founded the Bitcoin Magazine website and poured his knowledge of cryptocurrency into hundreds of articles. It was Buterin who first talked about Ethereum in a white paper that attracted other developers to join in the project's development. Today, he is the chief scientist of the Ethereum Foundation that develops and maintains the crypto-technology of the Ethereum blockchain. It was Dr Gavin Wood, another co-founder of Ethereum, that developed the specifications of the Ethereum Virtual Machine that is responsible for running smart contracts. Joseph Lubin, also a co-founder of Ethereum, later founded ConsenSys which focuses on creating decentralized applications. The team behind Ethereum have an impressive skillset and shared experience which helps place more confidence in Ethereum's future.

> In recent news, Ethereum has partnered with a Russian development bank. The bank and the Ethereum Foundation will work together to provide specialist training in blockchain technology and the Ethereum platform. The idea is to grow a strong network of Russian blockchain experts, moving Russia to the forefront of this technology. The bank will provide funding, which gives Ethereum stability. This will have a positive effect on the value of Ether.

So, the future value of Ether seems promising. However, to give you a balanced view, here are some possible issues with investing in Ether:

> Ether has no cap, so it is possible to produce endless amounts of Ether. As the supply is not fixed, any future supply restrictions are completely speculative. This is important, as asset prices are driven by supply and demand. This uncertainty of supply could represent a risk for investors.

> Ether is not actually a currency. It can't be used to buy any goods or services except on the Ethereum blockchain (or exchanged on currency exchanges for other cryptocurrencies). Its value is dependent on the success of the Ethereum network.

> Although unlikely, there is always the possibility that the Ethereum blockchain could be replaced

one day by superior technology. If this happened, the value of Ether would crash.

As with any investment, Ethereum comes with pros and cons. The value of Ether is largely tied to Ethereum's success as real-world technology. As Ethereum has recently displayed extraordinary progression as a new technology that can power thousands of different services and applications, it gives the impression that the value of Ether is set to rise. The choice is yours whether to take the opportunity to invest or avoid the risk.

## Chapter Summary

In this chapter, we looked at why investing in Ether has its advantages and how it can be a profitable investment. We also explored the risks of investing in Ether.

- Ether's sudden rise in value caused suspicion among investors. However, the increase in value is perfectly feasible, as it is an unprecedented technology that has the potential to revolutionize thousands of service processes.

- Some main arguments in favor of investing in Ethereum include the fact that it serves more purposes than Bitcoin, it is supported by several Fortune 500 companies, and it is being used by some financial institutions to streamline their processes.

- Other reasons to invest in Ethereum are that it is safe, the price is relatively stable, there is an incredibly skilled and talented team working behind Ethereum, and a Russian development bank recently partnered with Ethereum, which secures future funding. If a large bank is willing to invest in Ethereum, it indicates a positive outlook for the technology.

- Some of the risks of investing in Ether are that it has the uncertainty of its supply is a risk for investors; the success of Ether is totally dependent on the success of the Ethereum blockchain, and a more superior blockchain could render Ethereum obsolete. If that happened, it would completely devalue Ether.

In the next chapter, we will look at what the future could hold for Ethereum and its development.

# Chapter 11: The Future Of Ethereum

In this chapter, we will look at the future of Ethereum.

One of the most important changes in Ethereum's future will be the network's shift from a proof-of-work system to a proof-of-stake system. Before going into what this means for users, here's the key differences between proof of work and proof of stake.

## What Is Proof Of Work?

Proof of work is the typical protocol for most cryptocurrencies. Both Bitcoin and Ethereum use it. It works by letting miners mine the blocks by solving puzzles and receiving currency rewards after a block has been validated and released onto the blockchain. A miner is rewarded when they receive a specific proof of work – a system that proves they have been working on that specific block.

## What Is Proof Of Stake?

Proof of stake will convert the current mining process into one that is virtual. Miners will be out and validators will be in. This rewards those with stakes in the blockchain, or, in other words, those with holdings of Ether. Validators validate blocks by effectively placing bets on it. Once the block gets validated, the validator gets a reward proportional to the stake. Get it wrong, and the validator loses the stake. This system favours those with higher stakes.

The problem with this change is that those who mine Ether for profit will no longer be able to mine under the proof-of-stake protocol. The GPUs can be used with other coins, but it isn't really as profitable. Before investing in GPUs for mining Ether, it would be best to do some research to find out the exact date as when Ethereum will switch to a proof-of-stake system and therefore how long there is left to make profits from mining.

# Implementing Proof Of Stake

Ethereum will use the Casper-consensus algorithm. However, it won't be an overnight change. It will start as a hybrid system, with most transactions still done through proof-of-work mining. Every hundredth transaction will be done through proof of stake. This allows a test run to check the compatibility of proof of stake with Ethereum's platform.

But why switch from proof of work to proof of stake in the first place? The reason is that proof of stake comes with some key advantages:

➢ Firstly, proof of stake is far friendlier in terms of energy and cost. Proof of work uses a huge amount of energy, which costs a lot of money. By moving everything to a virtual environment, not only is it far cheaper, it is also more environmentally conscious.

➢ There is no equipment advantage for users. As the process will be completely online and virtual, the quantity earned won't have to depend on who has the best and most expensive machine.

➢ Although not a serious threat, as the possibility of it happening is very slim, the 51% attack exists with proof of work. The 51% attack is when a group of miners get the majority – or, over 50% – of the total hashing power. By using proof of stake, this threat is completely eliminated.

> It helps build an even safer blockchain. As a person's stake is on the line, it would encourage validators to only add good blocks in the blockchain, and not malicious blocks, as their invested stake would be at risk.

> Proof of stake actually speeds up the whole process.

> It also creates scalability on the blockchain.

So, how exactly will Ethereum move from proof of work to proof of stake?

Currently, the Casper scripts are being checked for bugs and any implementation issues are being ironed out. It will take time, but the main idea is to eventually make the majority of block creation done through proof of stake. To do this, the Ethereum network will pass through a phase that is being referred to as the Ice Age. This will basically make mining exponentially more difficult. The math puzzles to solve will become so difficult that it will reduce the hash rate and result in a slower blockchain. This will encourage people to leave proof of work and move to proof of stake.

Although this may seem relatively straightforward, there are some potential problems. The main issue is that some miners may not agree with this move and create a hard fork in the chain before the transition period to proof of stake. If this happens, the miners will continue to mine in the new chain under the proof of work conditions. This would mean that there would be three different Ethereum blockchains running. In addition to Ethereum (which would then be using a proof-of-stake system), there would also be Ethereum Classic (the chain that resulted from the last hard fork), and a new Ethereum proof-of-work chain.

One of the major discussions regarding Ethereum is its potential to overtake Bitcoin. People are getting excited about this possibility. But could this really happen?

There are possible scenarios in which Ethereum could feasibly overtake Bitcoin as the top cryptocurrency, but there are also scenarios in which it would never happen.

The factors that affect the growth of cryptocurrencies, in particular Ethereum, are the following:

> Having a strong community supports the growth of the blockchain, especially in the beginning, but it is important in all stages of the cryptocurrency. In the case of Ethereum, its community is strong thanks to the potential of smart contracts and the value people give the Ethereum network. Ether as a currency is purely there to pay for the services of the Ethereum blockchain, so the strength of the community depends on the existence of smart contracts rather than Ether. However, this doesn't mean much in terms of Ether value, as the demand for Ether will be there for as long

as people want to pay for the services of the Ethereum blockchain.

➢ In terms of what Ethereum provides, its potential is enormous. This will have a positive effect on the growth of Ether value in the future.

➢ Long-term goals are important for cryptocurrency growth. Ether has no cap, which could have an adverse effect on its future value. As more and more Ether is produced, its value will eventually deteriorate.

It is likely that Ethereum will become huge, thanks to its extraordinary capability to change processes as we know them. However, it is unlikely to replace Bitcoin. The reason is that the two exist for very different purposes, so instead of one replacing the other, they are more likely to become strong competitors.

In the end, the most important thing to the future value of Ether is the move from proof of work to proof of stake. This change will have a significant effect on the price, most likely a large increase. The reason for this is that moving to proof of stake will reduce the number of Ether produced per month, which will consequently lead to higher demand. As the demand increases, so does the price.

# Chapter Summary

In this chapter, we looked at possible future outcomes for Ethereum.

- Ethereum will shift its current mining system (proof of work) to a proof-of-stake protocol. This will be done gradually and will impact Ethereum in several ways. Miners will no longer be able to mine. The value of Ether could increase due to limiting the supply of the coin and due to the inevitable media attention this change will cause.

- There are several factors that foster success for cryptocurrency and blockchain technology. These are community, the number of applications, and its long-term goals. Ethereum has a strong community, an enormous capability of supporting thousands of apps, but no clear long-term goals. Overall, the future looks good for Ethereum.

Ethereum is often compared to Bitcoin, and many people wonder if Ether (Ethereum's cryptocurrency) will overtake Bitcoin. It is most likely that Ethereum and Bitcoin will continue as competitors rather than Ethereum replacing Bitcoin. The two have different appeals to different investors.

# Final Words

You've reached the end – thank you for sticking with me and learning all about Ethereum!

I wrote this book to condense my knowledge and research into Ethereum and bring you the hard facts, uses, and investment feasibility of this unique blockchain technology. After reading this book, you should have a much better understanding of how Ethereum works and its place in the world of blockchain technology.

From an investment point of view, I think Ethereum is one of the most exciting cryptocurrencies and technologies to invest right now. Whether you feel the same or not, I hope I was able to provide you with enough information for you to decide for yourself. Even if you decide investing in Ether is not for you, you should now have a firm understanding of the technology that looks set to change the way we do things.

Thanks again for reading my book, *Ethereum: The Ultimate Guide To The World of Ethereum*!

If you enjoyed this book, please take the time to leave me a review on Amazon. I appreciate your honest feedback, and it helps me to continue producing high-quality books.

# About the author

31-year-old Ikuya Takashima is a Software Developer, entrepreneur, investor and author.

Ikuya first entered the world of Cryptocurrency in 2014 when he finally decided to invest in Bitcoin after several years of following the online currency. Ikuya is now a Cryptocurrency expert & enthusiast with an impressive Cryptocurrency portfolio and investments in several Bitcoin & Ethereum startups.

Ikuya's latest venture is to share his knowledge and passion on the world of Cryptocurrencies with the goal of making seemingly complex and intimidating topics simple and easy-to-read.

In Ikuya's spare time he likes to read, travel and spend time with family and friends.

# Also by Ikuya Takashima

Cryptocurrency: How I Paid my $100,000+ Figure Divorce Settlement by Cryptocurrency Investing, Cryptocurrency Trading

(Available on Amazon)

This book covers the topic of investing and trading in cryptocurrency, and will teach you everything you need to know before you delve into this potentially highly lucrative world. You will learn what cryptocurrency is and how to decide which one to deal with. This book will show you the pros and cons of the various platforms for storing and exchanging cryptocurrencies and guide you neatly through the web of information out there about cryptocurrency trading.

At the completion of this book, you will have a good understanding of what cryptocurrency is and be able to make informed decisions about investing and trading them.


Bitcoin: The Ultimate Guide to the World of Bitcoin, Bitcoin Mining, Bitcoin Investing, Blockchain Technology, Cryptocurrency

(Available on Amazon)

The world has always run on traditional fiat currencies, which have been backed and controlled by governments.

The government can inflate or deflate the price of these currencies without any democratic involvement. This also meant a high degree of regulation and government scrutiny that led to manipulation, but then came Bitcoin.

Bitcoin is a decentralized virtual currency that is not controlled by anyone, and that doesn't require a third-party intervention. It was created by a figure known as Satoshi Nakamoto in 2008. His identity is still unknown, and he vanished from the online world a few years after introducing the world to the revolutionary technology of Bitcoin.

Bitcoin's value has increased over the years because of its popularity, and many people have made a lot of money from it. No central figure controls Bitcoin, but it's regulated by a peer-to-peer network that provides it with a functional base without the need of an external figure. Bitcoin is a democratic currency because it can't be influenced or manipulated by a few wealthy people for their gains and interests.

Most people have heard about Bitcoin and cryptocurrencies, but there is a lot of mystery that surrounds this terminology. Therefore most people are hesitant about investing in this lucrative currency. Bitcoin has almost become a buzzword in the last few years, thanks to its growing popularity. But the important question is, how does Bitcoin function? Is it a sound investment opportunity? How can you buy Bitcoin?

If you want the answer to these questions, then this is the book that you need. Bitcoin is changing the world, and it is entirely possible that in the next twenty years, it might become the currency that everyone in the world uses. Some governments, like that of Japan and Switzerland, are openly embracing it while others are strictly against its use.

Bitcoin is growing every day, and those who are in the game are already making thousands of dollars from it. So, if you want to understand what the hype is all about it, you have found the right book.

CPSIA information can be obtained
at www.ICGtesting.com
Printed in the USA
LVOW03s2019181217
560168LV00037BA/3400/P

9 781978 012370